THE S _ _ _
NEVER SLEEPS

Poetry from a Year on Four British Farms

Adam Horovitz

Illustrated by Jo Sanders

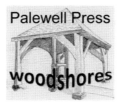

Palewell Press
woodshores

The Soil Never Sleeps

Published by Palewell Press Ltd
http://www.palewellpress.co.uk/

First Edition

ISBN 978-1-911587-05-7

A CIP catalogue record for this title is available from the British Library.

for John Meadley, expert herder
of poets and many other things.

Introduction

In late 2013 I was approached by John Meadley, chair of the Pasture-fed Livestock Association, with a proposal for a project. "Would you," he asked, "be interested in writing about pasture farming, and visiting some of our farms?" I was in the midst of writing *A Thousand Laurie Lees* (a memoir that pays particular tribute to the landscape of the Slad valley, and the way it has changed since Laurie Lee's youth) and my deadline was looming. I said yes, and didn't think about it again for months, as the book on which I was working took up full occupation of my thought processes.

John, however, didn't forget. He came back to me soon after that book came out and reminded me of the idea, pushing me to consider looking at the future of the British landscape in the wake of investigating its past.

His enthusiasm was infectious; clear of the other book, I became eager to explore areas of the British landscape that I didn't know, and to dig deeper into aspects of man's relationship with landscape and animals, under the surface of things of which I had only ever seen the surface before.

Growing up, I had a mythic sense of the landscape instilled in me; most of my understanding of its minutiae, of what made it work and what work it made, came from reading. John's proposal that I embed myself on four Pasture for Life farms over four seasons, and get my hands dirty, was intriguing, given how isolated and sedentary a writing life can be.

So four such farms were found willing to house a poet, in the Yorkshire Dales, Cornwall, Kent and

Wales and, in April 2016, I became the poet in residence for the Pasture-fed Livestock Association, rather to the surprise of some of the farmers in the PfLA, and, looking back on it, myself.

I visited these four farms over the course of the following year, keeping a written and photographic journal as I travelled. The poems in this book follow the seasons as I experienced them on the farms I visited, and they have a certain amount of narrative structure, with recurring characters who'd changed each time I visited. As a result, Spring is followed by Autumn, which runs on into Winter and then jumps to Summer. Given that the Brexit referendum happened in the midst of this residency, the final section of the book, which investigates the ethics, politics and future of farming, took on a new urgency in the wake of the changes that have been, and will be, wrought by that decision.

What makes these farms different is their decision to not conform to the post-World War Two chemical-driven farming consensus that has seen soil and food stripped of nutrients, and animal welfare suffer, in the name of remorseless productivity. Their commitment is to raise ruminant animals wholly on pasture, under the PfLA's banner of "Pasture for Life", with the attendant benefits to the animals, to the environment and to humanity that a holistic, nurturing approach to farming allows.

I am profoundly grateful to the farmers: Chris and Janet Jones in Cornwall; Neil Heseltine and Leigh Weston in the Yorkshire Dales; Nick Miller and Sarah Dickins in Wales; Fidelity and Martin Weston, and Matthew Lewis, in Kent. Their time and generosity made the writing of this book possible, and their voices are inextricably wound into the text that follows.

Despite our best efforts, it was not possible to arrange visits to a farm in Scotland, meaning that, regrettably, this book does not cover the entire island. For anyone wishing to read poetry about farming in Scotland, however, I can recommend Jim Carruth's *Killochries* (Freight Books, 2015) very highly.

Adam Horovitz

Contents

"To know fully even one field or one land is a lifetime's experience. In the world of poetic experience it is depth that counts, not width. A gap in a hedge, a smooth rock surfacing a narrow lane, a view of a woody meadow, the stream at the junction of four small fields – these are as much as a man can fully experience."

from 'The Parish and the Universe'
in *Collected Pruse* by Patrick Kavanagh

I Believed I Understood the Land

I believed I understood the land once, long ago,
a child running in his mother's footsteps, who gleaned
the names of birds that burst from the hedgerow,

who pulled up solid fronds of fern that leaned
out into his path to be sword and ploughshare,
imagined toys that soiled his hands and greened

the valley sunlight as he caught foxes unaware
when they bolted home across the failing pasture
spilled out below his house. I would not dare,

now, to say I knew anything of land. It has no master;
only people who strive to learn and understand
the minutes of it, and the hours. The earth moves faster

than we can comprehend, so seek a segment, find a strand
of it that you can love. Listen to the movement in one hedge.
Attune to it. See what it will give. Make no demand.

If you've listened, you'll know we're balanced on the edge
between oblivion and life and that the only charm
for our salvation comes in the moments when we pledge

to do no lasting damage, cause as little harm
as we can manage in field or office, city street or farm.

Spring

You'll Find Your Way

There's steam rising from the road
as we ride the quad bike
up narrow lanes between fence-topped
walls to the gate out onto Pikedaw.

I cling on hard, perched like a parrot
behind Neil, the dogs racing us as we
pass the erratic downward flow of tractors,
hikers and tourists in polished cars.

You know the grass is growing
when tarmac steams,
shouts Neil over his shoulder.
It's warm and wet. The perfect time!

We slide upward through moisture
rising to meet thin strips of white
clawed across a seam of blue.
I raise my face to watch the sun.

**

Beyond the gate, the quad bike
bucks and shifts on rough lanes
between rocks like a circus bronco.
I won't be thrown. Knuckles white

against my plywood seat, I twist
to the tune of Pikedaw. A grim
laugh bursts from my lips.
You alright? asks Neil.

continued

Spring, Hill Top Farm, Malham, Yorkshire

You know, I'm the first farmer
in a millennium not to farm this land
on foot. I'm two stone heavier
than my father was, at the same age as me.

At the peak, Neil points out
a steep incline down through rocks.
The farmhouse is down there.
Follow the walls. You'll find your way.

Pet Lambs

At the far end of the barn, away from the bull
which bellows forlornly as we pass, live five
hand-reared Blue-faced Leicester lambs. One, locked
into permanent supplication by front legs

bent as shepherds' crooks, hauls itself up onto wooden
slats to fix its gaze on us as we pass. The others
scuttle with weak enthusiasm around their pens;
Pavlov's lambs triggered by a bucket's hollow clank.

Aroused by the smell of powder, swilled in a bottle
until the liquid thickens into milk, they suckle
with a frenzy more avid than a calf's, their eyes
focused, determined to the point of madness.

They wallop into one other, suck at my watchstrap,
coated with a rime of milk-froth that has spread
from the bottle's suck-loosed teat. It's just
high enough to let them mimic the art of reaching

for their absent mother's swollen dugs.
One tiny Swaledale, too small to reach through
the barricade of wool, attempts to suckle at another lamb,
its black face vanishing under the press of bodies

until it's hauled tenderly into the farmer's lap to feed.
These are the lambs that wouldn't survive the wild,
says Neil, sat looking out across the farm. *The pets.*
I don't like to keep them indoors if I can help it.

continued

9

Spring, Hill Top Farm, Malham, Yorkshire

Look at the crooked one. When it was born
it was just led out on its side, with a stomach feed to it.
Still, there's newborn lambs out in the field above.
The Swaledale jerks in his arms. We watch it shiver,

shudder-legged, as it pursues the dislodged teat.
Neil shifts it on his lap, waits for the still air to quicken,
for skylark song and the rasp of suckled milk
                to fuse into a lullaby for sheep.

Permanent Pasture

There's owls up in Butra Barn, says Neil
as he hauls the gate closed over a wedge of rock.
*The RSPB have been ringing barn owl chicks
a while now. One was found dead in Lancashire
the other day. Serves it right for tekking a wrong turn.*

He points across fields, over the stony web of hill
to the distant barn. *These used to be youth hostels,
you know, for herds which drovers brought from Scotland
to fatten or to sell. It's why the walls settle in so tight.*
        A phone trill above our heads. *Lapwing.*

And look, a hare! It crackles like lightning
at the edge of sight, leaves its ozone quiver
in hanging heads of grass. *Fifteen years down the line
and the environmentalists were right.* Ungrazed,
the pasture's pocked with colour, a carnival of clovers,

flowers, herbs and grasses that raise their beaded
heads to the rhythms of the wind. A skylark, worried
at my heavy step too close, claps into the air like cannon-shot.
*Fifteen years of nature turning as it should.
Even the bird's eye primroses are coming back.*

Spring, Woodland Valley Farm, Ladock, Cornwall

Rooks

Fifty years ago, we had more rooks
than you could count.
They played havoc with my father's spuds,
so he went out one morning
and shot every single one.
The place was quiet after that.

There's no potatoes here now. Only,
in this raucous corner of the farm,
a woodland full of dark-winged birds
playing in the air, each dive
and throaty whoop a distorted mirror
of the children who come here
from schools, to learn the slower ways
of farm and nature – and,
out in the pasture, long free of crops
that can be raided by feathered clouds,
a balance of song that underscores
the scatalogical anarchy of rooks.

We have more rooks now
than you can count,
cawing and scrapping
in the high scrabble of trees
just coming into bud.
I like the balance, but not the noise.

Mob Grazing

i

Grass is a pump.
A piston working through the earth
taking carbon from the air
to sequester in the soil.

The cattle work this pump for us
each day as we fold them out
across the field, following the line
of the electric fence.

No, they don't like the wire.
Look how they butt each other
at the humming edge,
eager to reach new growth.

There's always one or two
who'll leap the moon
and risk its voltage
for fresh chicory, plantain, clover,

a taste of yarrow or deep-rooted dock.
It keeps them calving,
dock. Iodine rich. An anti-microbial
just growing in the soil.

It'll be three months or so
before they're back here.
This wasted patch will be in full
flower again after a hundred days.

continued

Spring, Woodland Valley Farm, Ladock, Cornwall

The parasites in their dung
should have died off at last.
We mimic nature as we move.
An electric wire for a season's shift.

It takes two days for pasture
to be reduced to this. Give them
a small area to boost their eating,
until, like Tantalus, they attempt

to stretch their necks beyond
fences. Look how they shift –
they know the charge is dead.
Hold that wire taut, it's time to move.

ii

I hold the wire. Skylarks sing
high in the serrated blue.

*It takes a quarter of the day
just to shift the fences,* Chris says

before he moves off down the field,
attaching wire to the teeth of plastic poles.

I turn to my phone, check Facebook,
new to this and bored of standing.

The wire goes slack.
Tighten up, Adam, or they'll escape!

Spring, Woodland Valley Farm, Ladock, Cornwall

The call from the far corner
of the field is carried in too late

on a tensile breeze.
One cow bounds over, then another,

then one more before the wire
is taut enough to put the others off.

Ah, damn, says Chris as I hide my phone
and he scrabbles for his.

*Janet, three of them are off
in the high pasture. We'll need the horse.*

Ashamed of my inattention,
I put aside phones and photographs

of sunlight on pasture, let go
the poet's tendency to wander

and hold the wire hard. I run
my imagination through it as electricity,

attempt to keep the remaining cattle
bordered in by thought.

Just hold it taut, calls Chris.
Hold it taut, and don't let go again.

iii

Here comes the cavalry of Janet
rising to the horse's trot as the hill
eases away beneath them.

The cattle shift into new positions,
guarded as teenagers caught smoking
out of their bedroom windows

as the cavalry of Janet sweeps round,
outflanks the herd and, with a gentle whoop,
halts all efforts to escape.

The three who made it across the wire,
away into lush depths of calf-deep
pasture, are nowhere to be seen,

gone over the hill's crest
into a wide blue of imagined
forever-clover, but the cavalry of Janet

bolts off after them as I pull the wire
taut and impenetrable, and plastic holding posts
are plunged into position like hasty infantry.

It takes mere minutes for the deserters
to return glum-faced and sulky to the last gate
left between hedge and electric fence,

the cavalry of Janet riding triumphant
in their wake, sun caught like a halo
on her wide brimmed hat. We shift

at her command, take up our places,
moving ourselves as the cattle move
to block all avenues of retreat.

The cavalry of Janet romps all deserters
out of the wider pasture and I run, flailing
wire and arms, to make a connection.

The fence goes live and cattle settle to its insect
hum, turn their heads down to pasture rasp,
slaves to their tongues once more,

as the cavalry of Janet waves her hat at us
in benediction, trots off in a parade of one
back down the hill, to the quiet of the yard, and home.

iv

Looking out later across Woodland Farm
from the one high hill, where birdsong's
cut short by the insistent whir
of a community turbine,
the land's laid out as a quilted map.
A rolling mesh of green and brown,
that, in the distance, shifts to silver, grey.

The closest quilt marks the patchwork
passage of the cows. They move like ink
across brighter greens, caught
between fences invisible to the naked eye.
Half the hill, up from the farmhouse,
has been stripped and muddied,
caked in dung and eaten down to almost nothing.

Further over, on another farmer's land,
sunlight blazes back up silver
from the panelled fields. No room for mammals;
they've been given over to the farming of the sun.
I'd be happier if they gave some space
to sheep or, better, cows, says Chris, rolling a weighted
pole down to the next section to be fenced and grazed.

Beyond that, grey streaks in the soil. A sculptured
set of hills that rise improbably against the sky.
Spoils from the clay mine they contoured
after Aberfan, then covered over entirely with seed.
Amongst this strange landscape, three stilled turbines
stand like monumental sentries, the skyline cut
between their blades into parcels

echoing the land the cattle graze.

Suppertime

Loosened by labour and a little local ale,
I lean into the kitchen table, ask
naïve questions about the taste of meat,
admit that I have never eaten it.

Felicity, the eldest daughter of the farm,
looks at me with an astonishment
normally reserved for cats
surprised in the act of being cats.

Why are you vegetarian? she asks.
I always have been, I reply. *I can't
digest meat now, would have to work
my enzymes up to the required speed.*

*I tried Turkey once, one Christmas,
drunk with friends.* Its wizened taste
did nothing for my festive mood.
You can't escape eating meat

on a pasture farm, Felicity says. *It's
almost as natural as breathing.*
She looks wistfully at her vegetables
while sister Jackie, determinedly thirteen,

balks and begs for sausages, will not
touch the chilli Chris has made.
He's not told them about the beans.
If they're good for feeding pigs,

continued

Spring, Woodland Valley Farm, Ladock, Cornwall

they're quite good enough for us,
he'd said as he scooped them,
mischievous, from the sack
at lunchtime. His son,

home late from school,
sits and wolfs his plate of chilli down.
That was great, he says.
What meat did you use?

Shifting the Sheep

As swallows skim cowpats for insects,
Sam, more prone to run at sheep
than stalk them, sinks out of sight
on command. Only his face,

like a negative of starlight, rises
from the pasture, which twitches
with his impatience. Just on the edge
of the shepherd's call, he dashes forward,

herds sheep over the imaginary boundary
between Sevenoaks and Tonbridge,
past the lightning-struck tree that marks it,
over an old brick sheep-wash,
used to cleanse wool until the war
brought nylons in its wake.

Sam, clumsy with enthusiasm,
runs hard into a ewe, fierce
as the orange stripe that marks
her back. She turns, head-butts him,
her eyes brittle, frustrated
as lambs bleat, leap and scuttle
away like startled salmon.

We close in around them, moving fast
to stop them breaking from the flock,
out of the well-trodden stream of grasses
that leads from gate to gate. Sam,
called off, slinks away. Glances back
and back again at victorious sheep.
Tugs hard at Matthew's whistled leash.

Spring, Romshed Farm, Underriver, Kent

Orphaned Calf

i

Two calves, striped
with a lick of green spray paint,
marked out as orphans,

lurk amongst the herd,
slip disconsolate from cow to cow
in search of milk.

One is clean:
Either not at suck or not allowed to try.
The other, filthy-faced,

wobbles eagerly
after a heavy-uddered cow,
grasps at a teat

whenever she stops
to scrape up high grasses. She does not
always move away.

ii

Dairy cattle would have no problem,
could be raised to four calves at a time,
then four again, then two as the milk
runs dry. These Herefords, raised

for beef, *are more willing to babysit*
than adopt and rear, do not always
take to joyful, needy interlopers
caught on the scent of milk.

Spring, Romshed Farm, Underriver, Kent

iii

The clean calf
does not recognize Fidelity.
Although she fed him
from the bottle yesterday,
it's still too long since formula
milk spurted from a rubber teat
    more fit for a lamb's
    mouth than a calf's
down its desperate throat.
The imprint has not held.

It runs from us, saucer-eyed, skips
past the reach of aluminium crooks.
Through the bellowed disapproval of the herd
it canters, then round a rotting tree trunk.
Attempts a thunderous imitation
of a lamb. We edge him, with the herd,
towards the gate's bottleneck.
The herd bellows, submits, squeezes
into a block of red and white,
from which the occasional head
shakes free in search of errant calves.

The orphan is just visible, moving fast
out of the reach of legs and udders,
streams of piss. Matthew closes in, mutters
as the calf bursts away like a bewildered seal
over the backs of tilted, precarious calves
at suck beneath their mothers.
We repeat the chase three times, then
corner him by the gate. It takes two crooks
to secure him at the neck, a wrestle
until the calf consents to feed.

iv

As soon as he tastes milk
the calf begins to suck. Matthew and Fidelity
catch breath, calm down.

      Their grip loosens

as white froth breaks
like surf on his lower jaw. His eyes slow
their rolling to a crawl

      as he succumbs

to the urgency of food,
barely blinks when the teat pops off the bottle,
is fished from his throat.

      Would you like to feed him?

Fidelity asks. She presses
the Appletise bottle into my hand, moves on
to find the other calf.

v

He follows the bottle,
tugs adamant after milk
and froth-stained fingers,
tongue coiled up
into prehensile rope.

I feed him until the scent
of me is caught in his nostrils,
till his eyes have flicked
off the madness
of flies and hunger.

Still he follows me,
butting at my groin
for milk I cannot give.
Now he's imprinted, says Fidelity.
A shame for him you're going home.

Trapped behind the gate,
he watches me depart.
I raise my hand, listen
as he hoots what I only hope
translates as a farewell.

Like a Sheep

Make a noise like a sheep, calls Matthew,
his voice urgent as the acid-tempered tegs

lurch in unison away from the gate again,
wheel round a lone beech to the field's centre,

ripe with the call of flowerless trefoil.
Last year's ewe lambs are an angry, greedy

brood of fleet-legged gossips, who yell
as they run from our steady pace, burst gaps

in our line like an anarchist cavalry.
Fidelity shouts *Meh heh heh*. The sheep

pay no attention. Matthew laughs. *That's
more like a cockerel*, he calls. *Again!*

The second time, it works. All ten tegs
skim in a furious cloud back up the field,

out through the gate, into the woods
where I wait to block the left-hand path.

The sheepdog, caught up in their mood,
runs them too close and fierce, does not hear

the sharp command to lie. Sheep pelt
into the woods, clamber through brash, crisped

bluebells, nettle. Matthew curses and gives chase.
As he rounds them up and calms the dog,

Fidelity hops a gate and runs the field to meet
the flock and head them off. I round a corner,

find one teg, exhausted, pressed into the verge,
haloed by yellow archangel, bramble strapped

across her rear. She pants at me but does not move
as I come close. Fixes me with one mad, yellow eye.

I call to Matthew: *A sheep's been hurt, I think.*
He scrambles down the hill, picks her up,

carries her gently to the field. On her feet again,
she stands and shakes herself. Turns. Looks sternly

at the dog, then ambles out to meet the flock.
Makes, to our relief, a noise just like a sheep.

Feeding the Pigs

A green shimmer of germinating oats
hangs over a raised lip
of ploughed earth, heavy
with the last weight of a well-timed rain.

A rare thing, says Matthew
scanning the clouds for skylarks.
And the wind in the right direction.
We've yet to hear the road

and will not, now the pigs
have seen us coming. They seethe
to the fence, a tumult of stripes
and high-pitched grunting,

press against each other
at the electric wire, tight-packed
and manic as commuters
waiting for the first tube home.

Twelve piglets boil at the farmer's feet
like a pan of water left too long;
they blunder, bicker, follow him to the trough.
He wets their heads to wet the food.

Only the boar is placid.
In the third enclosure, his hide
thick with wallow muck, he ignores
competitive, head-butting sows.

Orf in the Pasture

Lambing's finished in early May.
The grass came late this year. A wet,
relentless winter of submerged ground.

> *Half the rain,* says Sarah,
> *couldn't sink below the surface. Even so,*
> *the lambs did well.*

Though there's been Orf in the flock again,
the first case in years. Lambs lift it
from soil or from their mother, starve
as they suckle the corrupted teat.

> *So many cases 18 years back,*
> *when we first arrived.*
> *This time, just four succumbed.*

The farm, lost to layerage for decades,
housed sheep halfway to market
> *under previous tenants.*

> *The ground*
> *was robbed of nourishment, compacted,*
> *almost lost,*

> *the soil rife with Orf.*
> *So we looked for other ways of healing,*
> *beyond convention.*

continued

Spring, Pen-y-Wyrlod, Llanvethrine, Wales

Put homeopathy in the drinking water.
The sheep built
an immunity over 18 years.

A closed flock, safe.
What the vet brings is no cure.
It only halts infection of the teat.

All four dead lambs were bottle-fed,
born outside the loop of immunity.
　　　Only the rams are bought in for vigour;
to annunciate their different genes
from the backs of trailers, out over the low
slopes under Skirrid, later in the year.

In the distance, now, lambs
pitch like tarry barrels, leap up,
spring hardy after mothers
through late-grown, expectant grass.

We waited out the Orf. The other farmers
thought we must be nuts.　　　At first.

Post-Mortem

The flock were lambed indoors once, early on.
Mountain sheep taken from the mountainside
to dance, constrained, to the tune of supermarkets,
the need for larger lambs to fill their shelves.

We'd fed the ewes grain to bulk them out.
Three died, though they seemed vigorous.
So we called the vet. Who sliced skin open
to the flesh, pronounced it perfect, no trace

of excess fat. Peeled back the flesh to ribcage.
Again: *No problem there.* But beneath
the cracked-open cage of bone sat a white heart,
consumed with fat, the consistency of lard.

**

They're Black Welsh. Mountain sheep.
Built to be raised on hills in any weather.
We always lamb out now. Inside, they'd lamb
throughout the night. Born outside

the patterns shift. *Infection rates fall off.*
Sheep give birth till darkness falls, start birthing
later in the year. And shepherds can sleep easy
      in the busy arms of an auspicious spring.

Spring, Pen-y-Wyrlod, Llanvethrine, Wales

The Old Ways

Trevor Bevan says
that 'Guy Fawkes brings April Fool'.
A mnemonic from mountain foothills
        raised among sheep.

Lambs were born at Easter
                not eaten then.
The old ways corrupted, changed.
Religion called in to a lure of money.

On November 5th, in goes the ram.
He warms the stain of mountain mists.
Preaches his unpractised, pagan lust
        to a ready flock.

**

Our lambs, born later in the year,
rise to the immediacy of milk.
        Ewes ripe
with new-sprung grass and clovers.

The soil expels its dead each spring
as energy, pushed up through a maze
                of criss-crossed roots.
They resurrect quietly in the mouths of sheep.

It Came to Us Compacted

The hay field, bought at auction a decade back,
bids pumped up by rivals with housing plans,
was *ploughed relentlessly throughout the war.*

*It came to us compacted, full of dock. So we
made hay* of it, parked a gypsy caravan
in the corner of the field and let the biosphere build.

It's best, we've found, to focus on the soil itself.
Reduce inputs and let the field build up
               a city-weight beneath the sward.

**

*Worms beneath a field full of healthy cows would,
gathered up, weigh more than the cows themselves,*
says Nick. And: *plants feed many sugars to bacteria,*

are wedded *to a fungus layer* which spreads for miles,
exchanges information, levels out the losses in a field.
We don't just farm the top inch of the soil here.

A plough tears as atomic fire tears, wholesale.
Breaks up burrows it took ten years for worms to build.
Destroys the commuter routes of horizontal

traveller worms. Smashes the symbiotic satellite
networks of plant communication. They still lose
a little topsoil here. This is Wales; rain is ubiquitous.

**

Spring, Pen-y-Wyrlod, Llanvethrine, Wales

We walk the field, its permanent crop built high
beneath damp May sun. The turf's been slit
to let more air and water in. In the caravan,

a honeymooning couple pack away last flirtations,
get ready for the steady growth of married life.
A whisper of rain through trees. The soil does the same.

AUTUMN

A Sticky Prelude

Sheep gather in black clusters in the shade
of the farm's wild internal hedgerows, hang
like haw and blackberries to escape September's
last gasp of oppressive summer heat.

Some even worm their way beneath a stilled
tractor, glower out like trolls, stern eyes
visible through the haze rising from hot metal.
Only the crows and a distant 'plane speak

through this sticky prelude to autumn. Sheep
are silent but for the rasp of their mouths
on fading grass, the intermittent morse code
clang of curved horn on the tractor's rusted gut.

Smeuse Grazing

Sheep strip out
the lower reaches
of hedgerows

grown wild by choice
to house birdlife,
insects. Their hard

faces probe dark
holes for minerals
now grass grows slowly,

quest after methods
of escape
into wilder, unfenced

ivy paradises.
The woodland sings
to their stomachs

as grass turns
dry and musky,
still a little sweet from

the slow death of summer,
the quickened harmonies
of keen Welsh rain.

Cross-Purposes

In the pub, we speak at cross-purposes
about radical farming with two tourists
from Ohio. They praise miniaturisation,

machine culture, targeted fertilisers
reduced to minute levels to boost a crop.
We speak out against the plough,

in praise of fungal communication plates
beneath the soil. Explain how run off
is reduced, how carbon is locked in.

Our impasse continues into another round.
The froth of politics and the froth of beer.
Ohio is torn, as are they, between two

potential presidents they do not trust.
The only figure they are sure they know
in Britain likes to be photographed in pubs.

The conversation switches into anecdotal
safety zones. *Kansas,* we learn, *is flatter
than a pancake. It's been proved by science.*

Meanwhile, other farmers play skittles,
talk shop over the tock of the ball, the pale ale
paradox of pleasure and forgetting, cluster

with cigarettes in the cold night. Their cheerful,
cursive swearing punctuates dissections of the day.
Breath rises blue across the floodlit night.

Equinox on Caggle Street

Two workmen hammer at slates, crouched
on a cottage roof on the edge of Caggle Street.
The wind sifts sunlight through a net of cloud.
I know what he said but... one workman says,

raising his voice above the clatter of crows and hammers
but his sentence is lost as the wind rises to the hunt
over ragged hedgerows, carrying words on its flanks
to seed-scatter far beyond the farm's bounds.

A daddy longlegs lies dead in a cage of grass
pressed down by wych elm and field maple leaves,
the green-gold grave goods of summer's end.
I know what he said – but nothing comes

from the mouth of the hill to the cobnut casings
wrenched open by squirrels. Nothing but a weasel,
which stirs red lightning in the hollow lane,
carries the sun off squealing in its bloody mouth.

What he said but! What he said but!
An insistent cockerel in a nearby yard
echoes and distorts the worker's rooftop
fragment, refuses to finish his sentence.

In a hawthorn's spiked shadow, the secret
histories of escaped sheep are teased out
on dead bramble as a slower, low-down breeze
shakes insects free from abandoned bulbs of wool.

Autumn, Pen-y-Wyrlod, Llanvethrine, Wales

I know what he said but the roof falls silent
as men climb down their ladder and lunch
leaves condemnation and complaint
to the startled sibilance of departing birds.

Black Welsh Ram

The season begins with a ram, drawn
docile from his trailer into mountain-spun mist.

Skirrid sucks cloud into itself
as the first rains of autumn sing
summer into a waking memory of grass.

Water binds into glassy constellations,
builds a planetarium in the quarantine pasture

as the ram steps past a canine inquisition,
polite and cautious into its new universe,
fleece black as a condensed star.

Locked in, he proclaims himself welcome
to distant ewes, his bleat gruff as a flooded engine.
Alone for an hour, he rubs against gateposts,

explores fences for traversable wormholes
into parallel universes of hay and sheep.

Pasture, bloodlines, farmers, even
the tight watch-spring of the ram's horns –
everything is waiting for the rut.

On the Bridleway

Cows dawdle out onto the green lane
slow as tipsy teenagers all too aware
of the hours to fill before Friday night
steps up a gear. They gossip as they wander
through Samuel Palmer paintings, nose
into the ivied windows of the verge to brush off
flies, gathered at their eyes like clubland bling.

The heavy sweat of morning rises as steam
into glitter-ball clusters of blackberries
as high hedgerows flicker from red to blue
through a multitude of abstracted greens.
Cattle bell for calves caught in the undergrowth,
full of grass and stiff-limbed forgiveness,
tolerate Matthew's call and whistle, the wolfish
sheepdog's relentless pinch at their heels.

Stones turn beneath our feet, hoof-loosened.
We dance an avoidance dance as we follow the herd
down this shit-streaked bridleway. With the sun's
shift, we move from Palmer country into the Chagall-scape
shade of a crab apple tree, the cows a canvas of muscle,
heads dipped in pursuit of windfalls
                            which they snuffle up like pills.

Autumn, Romshed Farm, Underriver, Kent

Bloody Adam

The cattle won't leave the windfalls,
however much Fidelity calls.
Her shouts goad Sam into a frenzy.

He snaps at ankles. Twice, narrowly,
avoids a fecal crown, startles the calf
I'd bottle-fed last spring so much

it bolts into a hedgerow cage
of nettle, bramble, convolvulous
and saplings arched for capture.

Bloody Adam! says Matthew. I turn,
as does the calf. At least, he tries.
Come on Adam, you blasted thing.

He taps the calf with a plastic hose.
It shifts into deeper entanglement
while I relax, relieved I'm not at fault.

It takes five minutes with a knife
to cut the awkward calf a path back
out onto the hollow lane. Adam

skips back to his adopted mother,
crowned with tangled brash.
Bloody Adam's dressed for Christmas!

**

No apples left, except for muddy splatters
of sour white flesh buried in the path,
the herd accepts Matthew's call to: *Move along!*

It's a good pace, the Hereford stroll,
says Matthew. Just fast enough
in this unexpected mid-September heat.

He moves ahead. *Bloody Adam*? I ask,
catching Fidelity's eye. *We named him
after you*, she says with a small laugh.

And then, well. He misbehaved. A lot.
I watch the calf slither on a muddy bank.
Whisper *Bloody Adam* with a foolish pride.

Autumn, Romshed Farm, Underriver, Kent

Up the Line

i

Sheep froth like beaten egg white
in the long, penned line for health checks,
medication, a splotch of market dye,
squeeze cartoonish backwards, sideways,
over one another until all one can see of them
is wool, the marble-glare of many eyes.

*If there's fat at the tail, we've had them
far too long*, Fidelity says, briskly.
I press my palm into the nearest tail,
feel only bone. This sheep moves on
unsprayed into the open pen, where Matthew
wrestles with a fly-struck sheep.

He pins it against his legs, with brusque
sympathy, into the shape of a barber's chair.
The ewe stills slowly as Matthew's grip increases,
flails less and less, until the buzzer sounds.
Wool slips from its infested rear,
fouled snow from rooftops in a thaw.

ii

Not so agile in the line, the cattle huff
and bash their rumps against metal bars in
a slow choreography of polite resistance

until, heads locked into the bolus gate,
away from the crush of other cows,
they feel free to thrash at their restraints,

muscles shifting like tectonic plates against
the inevitable opening of mouths, the giant pills.
They're calm again as soon as they're let go.

We'd give them mineral lick, says Matthew, *but
some cows are greedier than others, stronger.
At least this way they're guaranteed good health.*

One old heifer, used to the line, does not succumb
to instruction or demand, refuses to move
behind the gate that leads into the run. We lean

into her tank-like frame. Still she does not move.
Matthew lifts her tail, pushes to get her underway.
The moment he lets go, she slams into the gate

I'm holding open in anticipation of one swift, final
sweep. Almost knocks me down. My arms shudder,
in tune with metal bars, to the music of her weight.

Bella in the Farrowing Quarters

Bella lies on her side in the farrowing quarters,
moans through the first flush of motherhood
as piglets wriggle around her like striped maggots.
They squirm for the nearest teat, latch on in silence.

Giving birth has softened her. In the field,
she ruled the dance for food and water
round the trough, clobbered Octavia into the tuskless,
disdainful boar as she dove in squealing.

Now, in the birthing purdah of the sty, her
orgasmic grunts are shyer, warn only of impending
shifts in body weight as she wards off pressure sores,
settles on cleaner straw, while piglets slip from her

like slow bullets. They leave raw streaks of blood
in straw as they work their way over her
back legs, drawn by the heady scent of milk,
their eyes ungumming in the half light as they crawl.

The other sow won't be such a pushover in the field now,
says Matthew, later, counting heads. *Eleven*, he whispers.
There were twelve before. One, born weak and wet,
has not made it over the pass across her legs.

Where's it got to? I ask, in slow confusion.
Matthew just looks at me, eyebrows raised.
I remember the power structures of the pigs, their hunger.
They're better recyclers than us, says Matthew.

Autumn, Hill Top Farm, Malham, Yorkshire

A Cup of Grain

Feeding chickens half a cup of grain
in the small paddock, two sheep,
kept here to recuperate, pelt
towards the drain cover where
seeds are scattered daily, bowl
chickens over in their haste.

The birds, outraged, bounce,
puff up their feathers, weave
and feint like outmatched boxers
against eight steadfast legs.
The just-released scrabble, noisy
to the interrupted feast.

Taking pity, I wade in, spill
chickens in my heavy-booted wake
to make the sheep move off.
Not far enough. They are lashed
to the illicit taste, the instant
sugar-rush that pasture lacks.

One cunning, squat-faced ewe
circles round behind me, attempts
three speedy raids, bleats a retreat
each time as we dance at arm's length
around furious hens, grain specks
and metal lid, until the feast is done.

continued

Autumn, Hill Top Farm, Malham, Yorkshire

I move off, and the sheep dive in,
lick in desperation at the husks.
I see them watch me in turn,
making sure I'm gone. At my feet,
hens take up a one-eyed-beggar stance.
They adulate the bucket till the gate is shut.

Sheep Psychology

Neil whistles. Whether to sheep
or to himself, it's hard to tell.
The wind has the hill in its mouth,
its multiple acoustics muffled;
a bulb of noise. Sheep surf over rocks,
uncertain of which way to move.

*I try to get them to go uphill
and they head down*, says Neil.
*Better at this time of year that they
go higher. The top of Pikedaw's
almost free of flies when it's this hot.*
He revs his quad bike, moves us

up the hill to herd them down. Sheep
scatter round us, engine-shy,
skip into reverse then climb the hill.
As they reach a higher plateau,
skylarks blast from the long grass.
Neil smiles, turns the bike for home.

The Family Farm

This is the family farm, bought in 1980
after thirty years as sitting tenants.
In time for interest rates to rise
      as farming incomes fell.

The old cowshed by the house is filled
with bunk beds, tourists too tired
to be aware they're being quietly farmed.
I came back to the farm full time

after foot and mouth, says Neil.
The cattle gone, sold when tourists
took over their winter home
to help prop up his parents' income,

only sheep remained, spread
over 300 acres, cropping pasture
to the knuckle of the Dales.
So I brought in Belted Galloways -

19 heifers and a bull. Bred
for this landscape. A hardy lot.
Part of a cattle conservation
      grazing scheme.

Fourteen years on, the herd
roams across a thousand acres
as the biosphere rebuilds
in their splattered wake.

The flock of sheep, reduced
by half and fed on pasture
instead of grain, *has turned*
a profit worth speaking of

at last. It's not conventional as such,
our method of farming. We used
to win the odd prize at Malham show,
bulk animals up to winning weight

with grain. Now the animals
roam as they were meant to,
only brought inside when sick.
They don't take so much weight

out on the hills, *but it's better*
for them. Better meat, without
chemicals dripped into the chains
          of food and wildlife.

Neighbours were a bit surprised wi' us
at first. P'raps they thought we thought
we were better than we were...
          That's mostly settled since.

In the field where last month's
Malham show took place, the only
prizes left are tractor scars in turf,
the silence of the summer's close.

continued

Autumn, Hill Top Farm, Malham, Yorkshire

A few hundred feet up, browsing
the last lush grasses, striped
Galloways are still astonishingly visible.
Countable from a mile away.

A sharp wind cuts across the hill,
slices through our jackets. Raises,
further up, rough, early strands
of the herd's thick winter coats.

First Mist

The glut of grass and herbs at summer's end
is waxed into the cattle's hides, which shine
like new-washed table tops. The sun's a blend
of mist, leaf-shadow. A dust of rain, fine

as silk, that turns pasture slick beneath hoof
and foot. The grey, close cloud sucks at solar
panels, then consumes them. Nothing is proof
against its descent. Monochrome stole a

march on morning with its subtle fingers;
grey suffuses grey until nothing's left.
Only the still and dew-fringed herd lingers,
visible, pushing at the fence like weft

ready for the electric wire's warp, its purr,
late grasses still ripening as the seasons slur.

Death and the Market

The bullock, at 30 months, is due
for market before the prices drop.
He skulks in the barn with a heifer
companion, also marked for sale,
to keep his blood quiet overnight.

She does not mourn or linger. The gate,
loose-tied, gives at her sideways push.
She breaks out, runs canny through the farm,
easily evades Patrick the German woofer's
loose, bewildered flap of arms. Heads

for the orchard, the chance to scrump
fallen apples. Remains uncatchable
until a grim-faced cavalry of Janet
marches her home, late. Death
and the market will have a week to wait.

Cider Season

A shudder of glass in the low barn.
Dozens of bottles stand on a worn bench
in military order, waiting to be sterilised for cider.
The light of a naked bulb salutes through them
hard into my eyes. Chris speaks
but does not break concentration:
Offers of apples just keep on coming in,
he says. *The season of ripening arrived*
quicker than expected. What was it
Keats said? Mellow fruitfulness?
He laughs, turns with an urgent rattle
back to the command of bottles, to the bench.

WINTER

Spoils

Cattle come running
to the hum of the quad bike,
the promise of hay sweeter
than this tired winter grass.

Here, at the top of the field,
in the cold rise above the farm
where the wind sits heavy
on the sun's shine,
grass grips close to soil.

Brambles flail over the fence lip.
Combs of bracken are pressed
into oblivion by eager hooves.
We have lured the bullocks here

away from the softer curves
of the farm's lower reaches.
The hay hurled from the trailer
is a bribe for their trampling,
a tribute. No weedkiller here.

The land fulfils itself
under the pressure of hooves
despite the old spaniel with a mucky eye,
keen to guard the bracken,

continued

barking and feinting rash challenges
to the cows as they rip hay apart
with limber tongues, test
their nascent horns brother on brother
in glass-eyed hunger games.

Today they are grass-starved demi-gods,
these bullocks, manoeuvred and conditioned
by greed into keeping down stray weeds.
All that spoils the pasture, corrupts the soil.

Wintering In

Before the haylage bale
is even free of tractor spikes
three wintering cattle have pushed
their rough, probing tongues

out like clumsy hummingbirds
through the feeding bars of the barn
after sweet, white, vinegary
stems of fermented grass.

Their eyes bloat with the satisfaction
of first lick, first chew. The cud's
been nothing but a dream since the last
wisps of hay blew into the fields at dusk,

scudding over skylark nests,
past trailers in a choppy lake of mud where
fair-weather pigs lay hugger mugger,
squealing softly for calmer waters and for spring.

Today, we pull the orange bale twine
out of the way of their unquestioning tongues,
lift up the hay until it fluffs,
expands, rises like abstracted bread.

We watch the bull stagger like a glacier,
steam curling through the ring in his nose
and the barn is suddenly golden -
a break in the clouds and the sharp sun

continued

has lifted hay into the scripture spectrum.
It is easy, somehow, to imagine
Saul sat in a Romshed field,
      straw between his teeth,

contemplating a name change
and the rites of spring
as clover grows quietly under the feet
of gods and beasts and men.

Worm Casts

Worm casts in the permanent pasture,
a roiling of soil into exotic, tiny castles
built to guard busy life beneath the lid.

None in the ploughed field, where children
do not stop to look; the sunken cityscapes
of insects, microbes, worms and roots

dissected by relentless blades, by light.

The Sickly Bullock

Nine months old yet wobbly
as a new calf on its hind legs,
one bullock has distanced itself
from the body of the herd.

We lure its compatriots with
a trailer full of hay to the next field.
They slide into the chase, red
winter coats slick as glacier ice.

Look back! The dog swerves
into wide pursuit, chases
the anaemic calf, who slinks
thirty mournful paces back.

The herd boil through an open gate,
spill into the wide new field. Only
the sickly bullock refrains, hugs
slow and sad to the nearest fence.

The dog is busy rounding up,
so I pat the bullock till he moves,
step from side to side behind
to keep him heading straight.

We reach a further gate. The dog
takes over, presses the bullock
through the tight-wedged herd.
We trap him by the trailer,

parked ready for evacuation.
He's lured, cautious, in.
The haylage's sweet vinegar
holds no interest. He leans

and looks at us, eyes milky-white
and weak. *Don't put water in.*
We'll need him ready
for any medicine the vet might bring.

Sheep in the Bramble

The sheep that strays to the pasture's edge
in search of fresher nutrients
risks finding only brambles on parting from the flock,
a prison of them coiled around tree trunks
where ivy's lush, seductive evergreen
boils upward like green fire,
whispering temptation and release.

Look at this one now, caught in a copse
at the field's edge, its fleece
crowned, and crowned again, with thorns.
It is stiller than you'll ever see a sheep.
Only its eyes move. They spin like marbles
flicked by a child, caught on camera and then
looped in the moment before connection.

See how it tolerates our approach.
Only a twitch of the hind legs signals
displeasure at the proximity of strangers.
Fidelity clucks at it, consoling noises
that stay both sheepdog and sheep.
She reaches in to find some simple
method of release. There is none.

Bramble has wound itself deep into wool,
as if the hedgerow is attempting
to absorb the sheep. Its stillness is
an aftermath of battle. Gobs of wool
brighten the bristle like early blossom
flecked with its own oils, and with blood.
      Fidelity unfolds her knife

shifts the sheep sideways, brusque,
determined. She cuts at wool and bramble –
any plant that stands in freedom's path –
tuts like a martinet dance teacher
lumbered with an awkward student,
calls the sheep affectionately angry names.
It moves only where she pushes it: pliant, unwilling.

Its eyes burn madder by the minute
as she slices, pulls and swears under
her breath. The dance takes her deep
into the bramble's reaches and only when
freedom seems a breath away does the sheep
begin to catch its tune, spilled in sharp
February light across worn pasture. It bucks,

startles in the thicket, risks deeper entanglement,
kicks the sheepdog (prowling closer now)
hard in the muzzle before it breaks away.
The yelping hound musters for a not-too-close pursuit
as, job done, Fidelity folds her knife in on itself
with a resonant click. Restarts her inspection
of hedgerows for yet more hungry, reckless sheep.

Bloody Adam in the Winter Pasture

Bloody Adam stalls in the field
as the sheepdog hurtles past

lean as a comet, sleek
through the sideways strike of winter rain.

Bloody Adam stands out amongst the maze
of bullocks. All are truculent, their energy

spent keeping warm in the low daze
of February. Wind carves the field

down to the bones of pasture
as Bloody Adam shifts like driftwood on mud,

wanting just to eat and move un-driven.
He stumbles backwards, bows his head,

refuses guidance. Except, when I reach my hand
out to brush the softness of his snout,

he leans in, sniffs and licks. A brief memory of milk
smeared across a vague, familiar scent, I think,

too ready for the luxury of attachment
in ways more numinous than by a name.

Storm

The willow on the lake island has split.
Half of it has been felled in a high wind, its rotten
base exposed. Two stems that grew together
have been bent apart by the storm's formless yell.

The summerhouse, spun to face the trees,
creaks on its wheelbase as dry-whipped
leaves dance paso doble around it
preparing for battle with the sky.

The whole of the farm is rounded up into eddies.
Even the sun appears only in a whirlpool
flash of cloud. We heard nothing of the tree.
It fell through this forest of noise,

this scattered jigsaw of wind that picks
voices of cattle up and drops them
in on us from impossible directions.
Who heard it fall, we wonder, *and how far away*?

Sheepdog and spaniels dance oblivious
in the courtyard, as if the wind has climbed their tails.

Winter, Hill Top Farm, Malham, Yorkshire

Walking the Bounds

i

The lane from the farm
is worn to a slippery sheet
of lichen-patterned stone
by foot, by wheel,
by water and by wind.

Lichen cleaves to stone, white
as the snowdrops bell-trembling
in furtive imitation of distant sheep
amongst last summer's
dead grass, sour in the verge.

Lichen's spot-picked clean
by a blade of February wind
that scythes along fossilised
desire lines of stone
      on stone
           on stone.

ii

This is a land of territories
laid out in keloid scars of stone

a place of pasture clusters
parcelled up amongst endless walls

that mimic the sheer horizons
patch by patch – the stark
bone-jut of lichen, moss luminous
as fresh pasture waiting for the graze.

Even the smallest rocks in the walls
look like the dales they rolled out of,
these hills that dance and keen like clouds.

Winter, Hill Top Farm, Malham, Yorkshire

iii

A dog, guarding chickens,
bounds onto the wall
to yell at me as I pass,
heading for the stile
over the way to Pikedaw.
It skips in circles across its chain
in demented, protective fury,
each bark repeated
by an invisible companion
on the far side of the barn
(I cannot tell if it is echo
　　　　or another dog).

The beast I see knows
nothing but the excitement
of defence, of barricades.
I suppose that to it I am
little more than stray scent,
an interloper roving between walls,
until, amused by its urchin thinness,
its ragged black coat, its shaggy
silhouette against a clipped grey sky,
I bark back, become
　　　　threat and arrogance.

The dog heaves forward
to the limits of the chain,
swings angry ropes of spittle after me
as I move on, fury following me
in zig-zags along dry stone walls
until all voiceless, territorial anger
is carried off by the sober
rush of a boundary stream.

iv

Rising step by step
on tongues of stone
into a westerly blast come
over the hill from Settle, I see

a calf pressed to the inner wall,
as if stone were its mother.
It skulks from the wind
far from the scent of milk,

stretches for its haunch
to lick itself warm,
the tendon in its neck
a vivid ridge of rock.

Winter, Hill Top Farm, Malham, Yorkshire

v

There's a sheep splayed by the open gate
of the hay barn below Pikedaw,
its hind legs skewed on stone,
tongue bloated, jaw set
like an emoticon, insouciant in death.

I lean in to photograph its number for the farm,
pull back from the mephitic
shock of blood
pooled in its empty eye,
like sour rain in a tarn after a storm.

Inside the barn,
checking for other deaths,
I find an ossuary of horns, curled
tight as snakes in the sparse,
late-winter remains of hay,

turn back and duck (this place
was built for animals and shorter men),
surprise a crow mid-sip, its blunted
talons hooked into the dead sheep's horn.
It startles, sprays blood

across wasted muzzle wool,
lifts itself bitter onto the wall
and calls uproariously for me to go.
There's nothing here to use for cover.
I must leave the sheep for birds. Head on up the hill.

Winter, Hill Top Farm, Malham, Yorkshire

vi

the hill's a moonscape of greys & browns
           – cattle far-flung as astronauts

rain runs varicose through clouds
           as walkers float downhill

gravity compromised, wind-lifted
           words flung on stone

their mouths set in silent promise
           of the coming sun

Winter, Hill Top Farm, Malham, Yorkshire

vii

The light, when it arrives,
         hurls itself across hills
in hallucinatory episodes.

Grey becomes green becomes brown
becomes green becomes stone and grass
and grey and dark shadows under eyes of stone
blink and lift themselves heavenward.

Walls pulsate with light and disappear, reappear,
heave across the sharp rise of the slope.
Hours slip by in moments, shift Pikedaw
through night and morning and afternoon then

back to night again, the hill a junction
of blood and light and unspooled time.
         I have walked
a thousand years in a hundred yards

and only the cattle-call to calves
has kept me rooted in the moment,
in the breath of this cold February morning
that bites at my eyes like retracting tears.

viii

Feet unsteady in the rutted
turf pools where marsh and hoof
have met in implacable pursuit of the last
possible tender stems of grass
      to survive winter's bitter marinade,
I slip into the hill's thin-aired suction rhythm,
clambering awkward across exaggerated
jigsaw footcasts of Belted Galloways,
staggered by the deep archaeology
      of their steady, certain ascent
up the seam of the hill,
where limestone meets millstone grit
in a rush of different plant life,
swollen out of the variance of acids
      antiquity has built into the soil.

A few cows appear over a lip of stone
like fuzzy humbugs just extracted
from the sofa's depths. They peer quizzically
over boulders, shift into defensive patterns
      around their awkward, hairy calves
as the herd appears behind them
at the glacial pace of cautious, semi-wild
creatures in an environment that has
worked through their marrow for millennia
      has become a music rising in their blood;
this pasture where curlews and oystercatchers
pass like semi-quavers, and skylarks rise
in startled crescendo from grassy nests
into a sky once more shadowed
      with the threat of rain.

Winter, Hill Top Farm, Malham, Yorkshire

ix

A sheep skull's pooled in the grass
     like a splash of milk
picked clean of cream.

     Under the white,
a seam of blue pulses
     as if blood runs beneath the bone.

Better that crows and insects
     have their way up here sometimes
said Neil last night, resigned

     to death, to the order of things
that cannot be easily managed
     or carted from the hillside

fifteen hundred feet
     above sea level, in a wilderness
of pasture, stone and blood.

     I pick up the separated horn
and pocket it as clouds
     rush past, unseeing

on their swift commute
     to Skipton, littering the hill
with charged brigades of light.

x

Balanced   on the giddy edge of the hill
I watch the sweep of walls
       shadow the swell of dales

surrounded by cautious,
disinterested cattle as they consummate
their endless regurgitated relationship

with herbs and grass.
Sheep startle at my slightest movement,
         like children

balanced in a vast playground
expecting an   endless
     game of tag.

Balanced.   Acre upon acre
of grassland interwoven
   with herbs and clovers,

     the land
bound tight into itself
       to hold the soil.

Carbon presses upward
carrying the weight of growth
     as Pikedaw settles

continued

Winter, Hill Top Farm, Malham, Yorkshire

into the insectile overtures of spring
        and calves stand to attention
    while time shifts up a gear

and a tractor grinds gnat-like
        on a distant lane.
Balanced   between wildlife

    and the need for food.

Winter, Hill Top Farm, Malham, Yorkshire

xi

down dale, rain-bitten –
    wheeling along

hard-pressed
    tyre tracks among rocks

        quad bike bridleways –
        the grass as slick as wax

counting distant cattle
    by stripe after stripe

    as clouds shift into sheep
  & back to cloud

        a distant peregrine pricks
        at the great stone scab of Malham Cove

the rhythm of my feet frenetic
    amongst rubble as hills blur

  into tarmac & houses
    & tourists who squeak

along pebbled pathways as
    order is built out of the monument

of the hill, a base camp
    at the foot of

    this great patchwork map
of stone   on stone   on stone

Winter, Hill Top Farm, Malham, Yorkshire

xii

In the farm kitchen, I shake off rain.
Hang traces of the day on a busy hook.
The old sheepdog tilts its head at me,
begs for scraps of scent as I sit and scratch
between the twin stars of its eyes – one blue,
one brown. As different and as close together
as Pikedaw and the wandering sky.

I am unsettled within doors. The light is
still and unbending. I carry the memory
of death in my mouth, the sheep's number
stings under my tongue. Leigh boils the kettle,
offers tea and normality as her daughter
laughs in the other room, roots through
imaginary landscapes where everything is living

and cannot die. Neil opens the door, brings in
a bolt of winter with a laugh. *A good walk?*
he asks, casting the contents of his pockets
on the table like bones. *I saw a dead sheep
by the hay barn, a crow sipping at its eye.*
He stops. Looks sad for a moment. *Ah,* he says.
I wondered if she'd mek it through to lambing.

*Did you see her sister under blue plastic?
I kept them round in hope they'd see it through.
They were old. It's hard living, up on Pikedaw.*
I open my iPad to find him the number of the ewe,
swipe my fingers over blood-specked wool.
A coldness settles in me. Not sorrow as such; more
my veins rebuilt as walls, learning the need for stone.

SUMMER

4 Minutes 33 Seconds

Almost asleep beneath a lippy bulge of wall, I listen for the landscape's orchestra of supposed silences: the litany of sheep; the creak of a cow's tongue as it pulls at high grass, risen from this tight soil like an inverted dream of rain. A percussion line of startled birds far up the lane divides earth from sky, opens into an unstrung Gore-Tex hum of distant tourists sleepwalking over rocks. Insects, grass and water hiss in harmonic shifts. Somewhere, the farmer sits at the keys of the land. He listens to the field's cage, his fingers, for these few minutes, still.

The High Hay Shivers

Gravity reasserts itself
    as heat in the summer
    pasture beneath Pikedaw.

The high hay shivers.
    All else is still, or shifts
    so slowly that movement
seems an impossibility.

Cattle & bare rock
    climb indivisible
    towards the sun

as it carves silver and water
    onto the wings of birds
    & the hill folds itself
into doughy shadow.

The breeze is stiff with pollen;
    with the disembodied
    migrant voices of sheep.

**

Summer, Hill Top Farm, Malham, Yorkshire

In the distance, a tractor
pinches and pokes at

black wads of bound hay
with blunt, mechanical delicacy

      perches bales like sushi
      bound for a winter table

      on its trailer, then lurches
      down the rough lane

as birds shake themselves
from the wall, swagger

in erratic fury up
into an oblivion of blue.

Summer, Hill Top Farm, Malham, Yorkshire

Maggot Patrol

Gate squeal and the low growl of an engine.
We roar through the fields on maggot patrol
as if we've ripped through the boundaries
of reality, arrived muddy-trousered
in a buddy cop movie's opening scene.
We follow suspect sheep as they scatter and bleat
in guilty staccato to the far corners of the field.

Riding shotgun on the quad bike,
I'm on the lookout *for mucky backsides,*
where flies have landed and laid eggs
in deep nests of shit-encrusted wool.
Maggots'll take a lamb in two days
if we don't catch them, says Neil. He turns fast
around a rock the lambs have leapt across,

points to one, rear end shaved like a poodle
down to its nimble legs. *We caught him just in time.*
I spot a lamb running, its arse dried black,
shout an alert. Neil spins the wheel. I cling on,
lean into the turn as he gives chase. *He's clear*
for now, but I'll keep tabs on him, he says.
Moves on now every animal's been checked.

In the third field we find a cow, who'd calved
just yesterday, pressed against the fence,
alone. Neil stops, rises on the bike, inspects the field.
There's no sign of any calf. *We'd better find it!*
Even though that udder's seen some use.
The cow chews at the hedgerow, oblivious
to the revving of the engine and our nerves.

We find the calf reposed in a pool of high, lush
grasses, still shiny from its mother's tongue.
It raises its head in dazed greeting, perhaps
hopeful of an injection of fresh milk.
Neil inspects it tenderly from head to genitals.
It's a heifer and it's fine, he says, as her mother
shifts to face us, bellows a caution down the field.

We step back from the calf. Mount the bike.
Return to maggot patrol.   Move swiftly on.

School Visit

i

Seventeen children from a city school
romp through the field, their laughter
tangled, in the valley's brisk echo,
with the playful bark of dogs.

Hush, calls Chris. A newborn calf
stands lonely up ahead, beyond the safety
of the electric fence. Its trapped mother
lows alarm at the diluted scent of wolf

amongst this city-awkward mob, most
unused to open spaces. She pushes up
against the fire of the fence, followed
by the herd, horns raised ready

for defence. In erratic waves, a silence
falls. The calf ducks back beneath
the wire as children gather, whispering,
into something that passes for a herd.

ii

The dairy herd arrived in calf.
New to the farm, they gave birth
in dribs and drabs from February
to the end of May.

At ten weeks old, the eldest
stand solid by their dams,
reach up eager to the suck,
as younger ones teeter

on the edge of growth, still
small enough to slip
into the summer pastures
they can't yet browse.

Nine months gestation, says Chris.
It wasn't possible to tell at first
when they'd fall due.
The city children following him

start naming calves.
Let's call him Inky – he looks like
Rorshach from the Watchmen film.
Chris turns. Looks them in the eye.

Don't name the little ones, he says.
Next year they'll all be born in April.
Easier to see, if they're raised together,
which ones go for meat.

If one might grow strong enough
to be a breeding bull.

iii

Down from the graze, into the slow
tangle of thirty-year-old woodland
the children stumble, stepping nervous
across electric wires pressed with a stick
          into a lazy V.

They follow the path through crisp
ghosts of bluebells to the heart of the wood,
stepping down bramble, their feet
unsteady on wet moss and broken
          fungal branches.

Chris presses on ahead, calls out warnings
about rabbit holes. He beats the high
nettles back with meditative ease.
This was bare land after World War One
          he calls across the trail.

The wood was used for industry when U Boats
fenced us in and held up trade. It seems,
now, as if the woodland was never lost.
Trees break and rot and grow again
          from the mulch of themselves.

Littered across the wet path, children
stagger through undergrowth
pick out long sticks for the barbecue,
hoist them on their shoulders like soldiers
          marching home from a forgotten war.

iv

The next field
 is a labyrinth of grass
cut for haylage,
 laid out in circles
like an Iron Age fort.
 Children run the maze
their feet sticky
 with washed-down clay,
race the rise of colour
 in the fields
against the tide
 of history's run-offs,
up from oxygen-starved
 soil at the woodland's edge
and down again
 to the hedgerow
where the blues of spring
 give way to a slow
pulse of purple: campion,
 herb robert, foxglove,
huddled hugger mugger
 in dew-wet early evening
colour charts of green.

v

A scar in the woodland.
Ditch. Posts. The river fenced.
Children scrabble over springy
walls of new-cut saplings,
       footing uncertain.

Their laughter booms back
at curious angles over still water,
moving water, out of dense
       triangulated thickets
of light-starved, hopeful trees.

Space here for turbidity gauge,
water quality sampler, testing
      for pathogens, dissolved
oxygen, carbon, potassium,
sulphates. Space for the beavers,

returning soon. This will be
      a fenced off lab to help us prove
that they prevent flooding,
fuel the abundance of bird life, fish life.
Engineering space for the engineers.

      Fish splash in the lake.
A dog yaps in the undergrowth.
Children seethe off in packs,
search out all the possibilities
      of the waiting wood.

The New Dairy

The milking parlour sits stark as a scar
on the farm, new-raised on the run
where last year one bored heifer
bashed her way out of loose-tied
gates to freewheel through
farmhouse gardens for a giddy day.

The herd has changed its shape
and colour since, to suit the parlour's
taintless shine. Columb blasts floors
with a hose each morning before
the cows arrive; again as milk is drawn.
Now he nudges four cows firmly into stalls.

We're testing the ground, he says
as he flips the switch on the squat,
robotic, mobile milking pump. *So far
we're getting 12 litres, 'though that'll increase
when milking moves to twice a day.*
The vacuum pipe flails like an octopus

as he attaches greedy tentacles,
reaches cautious up to the udder
from the wide channel three feet
below the cows. *It can get messy
down here,* he says, laughing, as one cow
raises its tail like an elephant's trunk

continued

to release a waterfall of piss.
Again, Columb reaches for the hose,
one eye on the cow being milked.
It shifts and settles to the suck
as he sprays urine into narrow chases.
It takes heat out of the building too.

Cows shuffle to the water's music.
Milked out, they're separated
from the tubes, respond in placid
tones to the lonely bellow of the bull
in a nearby barn. Columb sprays
iodine and glycerol on their udders,

his gloved hands delicate as he dabs
excess away. *It keeps them supple.*
He speaks with easy passion as he works,
hands moving between animal and machine,
soil and water. Takes each for what they are.
I'm glad we bought a low-yield herd.

He pours milk into a deep bucket, hoses
concrete, raises bars. The cows are released
into a pool of sun. *I can milk at 7am,
not 5,* says Columb. *As much as I like milking cows
there's always other things to do.*
        On the farm.   *In life.*

Raw Milk

Milk, ten minutes fresh
> from the udder,

spun like candyfloss
> at the bucket's rim.

Columb thrusts a cup
> below the crust of cream.

Have you tasted
> *milk this raw before?*

It melts on my tongue.
> Sweet. Warm.

I suck at the cup
> till all but a ghostly

filament of froth
> is gone.

High Pasture

With distance, there is oneness. A uniformity
of green from the far side of the farm, my vision
blurred by hard, bright five o'clock light as
July clouds peel back. The sky burns blue

into my eyes, masks the true depths of the fields.
A dry start to the year. It's been good for flowers.
Fidelity strides from the gate into the high pasture
that spreads upward to a cluster of young oaks

and the field opens up before her like a bruise.
A shiver of vetch on the surface, its wine-dark
stain held high among grasses, hides craters of trefoil,
their yellow slow to rise into immediate sight.

Bound in amongst this: self-heal, knapweed,
tares like delicate, abstracted peas.
Crickets and bees drown out the rush of cars
as we wade through a Van Gogh sunset canvas,

the field bent by our feet into heavy brushstrokes,
seeds scattered into infinities at every step. The meadow
sings like a universe beneath us. Below that
a multiverse, where almost nothing can be named.

Cut Hay

i

The just-cut hay's still clammy
at the cold edge of the field.

Matthew stirs it with his hand
until the air is stiff with pollen.

The sun rises
to its bleaching angle

as we wade through grass
spun into the ghosts of waves.

**

Nearly ready to be turned
by the tractor

then rowed and baled.
Just enough moisture

for the fermentation,
that's what we need.

A bit more time to dry.
Can't let the bales

distort under the weight
of wet. They're heavy as it is.

**

Summer, Romshed Farm, Underriver, Kent

Summer itches
under bone-bleached grass

where small blue and yellow
stars wait to be pressed

into silage film, for the season
to be locked in vinegar.

ii

When the machines arrive,
they suck the field up into wet bales
bound with orange twine,

lift them into a vortex
of green clingfilm to spin and seal.
The plastic hums like a starship,

hypnotic, endless, as it binds
the grasses into cycles of fermentation.
A hundred bales exactly.

Just what we'd hoped for.
The field is naked as an asteroid,
stubble white and close as dust.

Bloody Adam at High Summer

He is solid mass now. Last year's
feeble calf come slow to the call of milk

is Bloody Adam no longer. Just Adam,
boisterous in the herd, decorated

with the same medal-rack of flies
that shift like mercury in the slow heat

across every nose. Almost wild at last,
he comes cautious to my proffered hand

as his brothers watch dispassionate
in a tail-flick line, their heads bent

like curious children waiting
for a stranger to hand out coins.

Only when I lie down in the pasture
to take photographs of his brothers' bobbed heads

does Adam come close, his nose pressed
against my trousers, working out

a line of scent along denim ridges
from shoe to belt, in tender inquisition,

until the cautious spaniel barks
in alarm and chases him away.

Summer, Romshed Farm, Underriver, Kent

Leaving the field, I turn to watch
the herd press into a scrum

as Adam rises onto the back
of one of his brothers, then sinks

into the mass of flesh and muscle.
One last playful bellow   and he's gone.

The Soil Never Sleeps

The Abattoir

i

And here is where the intelligence
of grass is harvested, here
in pale, clean rooms
lined with jaws of metal
that smell of bleach, confusion.

A little man with old eyes
leans on concrete, talks of pelt pullers,
the consistencies of fat
preserved by stripping hides
from bottom to top

here in the hard-truth room
that runs unsteady underfoot
with channels cut to ferry blood.
A vegetarian? he says.
What the dickens brought you here?

I've come to see if I can understand,
I want to say. Instead I listen and,
almost mute, enter the exhibition room
where marbled sculptures hang
in cold companionship.

Like distorted globes they're marked,
all fourteen, with archipelagos
of flesh and fat. No weak, pink
plastic packages these, laid
like fancy bricks on supermarket shelves,

continued

but engines stripped of their facade
evolved to turn grasses, herbs
and flowers into weight.
Here is the truth laid out
in a sticky braille of ribs:

"...the dead become the intelligence of life.
Where the tree falls the forest rises."

ii

The world could turn to our survival
if we let it, working hand in root
    with the shift of seasons.
The whole of history and myth,
back to the first primordial split cell,
    lives as fragments in every field.
    The soil is restless.

We are born of compost.
Even our breath is history. Wind
    carries finite echoes of the dead;
the soil, an infinity, in mineral traces,
on fungal communication lines
    below the earth, stem to stem
    to everything that lives.

The measure of kindness on a farm
can be found when farmers deal with death.
    Some sympathies are cruel.
Blake's rose was surely sick of mankind's
collective refusal to believe
    that they are part and parcel
    of the land they breathe.

iii

It is not enough to say that 'it tastes good'.
What does it taste of? Cheap cane sugar
and reconstituted fat, or the depth and breadth
of a certain field, ripe at high pasture,
where the farmer's ploughed nothing, or just
pricked the soil to let more water in?

Nature is messy in its exactitudes,
but there's no need to be afraid of it. The weeds
growing from the field's edge are harbingers
of a soil's health. A cow with wagtail groupies
in its hoof prints, eating leaf-hoppers,
is a cow not eating poisons to pass on to us.

We built the inhabited world as a farm
over millennia. If we deprive the woodland
ruminants, which help us manage it, of trees, if we
whisk up soups in chemical vats to tame the weeds,
we strip the landscape of its language.
Make a bowl in which to harvest storms.

iv

There are always choices to be made. To eat,
or not. To live. To help others do the same.
If you believe the myths (again, your choice),
they tell us that to choose is inevitable, that some
choices may be wrong. It does not matter what
the myths are, more how they're interpreted. So,
let's say for sake of argument (this being Britain,
apparently still driven by such things), that God
made us as animals and then warned us off (or
pushed us toward) knowledge, in a farm. Then,
in a fit of fury, decided that we knew too much
and shoved our mythic forbears naked from the field.
Does that mean we are no longer part of that ideal
expanse? Not from where I'm sat now, looking
out over a valley half folded in on itself by trees,
growing fast in place of pasture, where apples
still grow in hiding and the knowledge of the sheep's
mouth lies buried deep beneath balled humps of grass.
Was it wrong for the farmer on the far hill to turn his farm
over to racing horses? To let this steep pasture, rumpled
as a still-wet shirt that's not yet hung, grow wild
while, on the close-cropped plateaus where the valley
spreads softly into habitation, out to roads, delicate
equine ankles are spared the risk of turning? No.

continued

And yes, to a degree. Though it's a selfish thought, I can
only just see across the valley to the pub, which is hidden
at all turns by tops of trees. In my childhood the village
was laid bare across a distant, lightly wooded ridge
and specks of people moved across the land, constant
as ants in pursuit of errant cattle and bewildered clouds
of sheep. The land laid out below me now sighs
with the erupted mystery of a sea of leaves. Birds rise
from the green like leaping fish. Fathoms deep, below
the measure of widening trunks, the soil rests with one
eye open, watches unblinking the eager, endless,
                    recycled blur of busy lives.

v

What I, in my moderate wealth,
commonly regard as hunger
          is nothing of the sort.

It is a craving for taste;
a salve to spread on tongues.
A monoculture built from the rot of greed.

True hunger begins at the roots
of want. I have felt its brief touch,
elusive as the rasp of soil on my teeth,

while eating a sandwich, made
of just-baked bread and local cheese,
my hands half-cleansed of toil   and the field.

vi

Nature turns to the pace of growth,
        the pace of falling.
However swiftly some new machine
      can shrive plants from soil

grass will still stretch out to the sun
      only as quickly
          as the tick
      of its internal carbon clock allows.

There is no easy fix to make the speed of rot
      pick up its ragged leaves,
its colonies of febrile insects, steady worms,
and run beyond the measure of the season's turning.

Time is the only thing we have to give.
           Time, and the unfussy application
of hand to soil to mouth to calf to apple to egg and on
      into the microscopic multiverse of soil

where all the sciences work as one
to generate the kind of heat
      beneath the earth
that I'd expect of a phoenix's rebirthing flame.

vii

This abattoir on the edge of town
will soon be gone. The owner's
sixty-eight and has no sons.
All the small places where care is taken
to separate pigs, who'll only fight
if mixed in with another clan, or lead
sheep and cattle gently to their death,
are being replaced by the vast machinery
of buildings far removed from mercy.

**

Don't write anything bad about us.
His handshake's mercilessly firm.
I assure him that I can't. I cannot,
even now, removed from that place,
determined as ever to not eat meat.
Although I can still see the friendly goats
in their pen under the blossom-heavy orchard,
and remember the way they greeted
both us and the sheep we brought
with equal fervour, I can also see
tender hands easing them
       back behind the lines,
never showing once the power
of their grip, as firm as death itself.

**

Grasses churn within beasts, are expelled,
become soil and grow more grass.
Animals, too, shift between these states
of being. Humankind, an animal itself,
for all that we may tell ourselves
that there's no chain, shifts with them.
We eat, and are eaten in our turn.

Context

Grazing animals are a tool,
like fire. If you are asked
to light a fire, would you burn
the house or warm the room?

A few sheep. A small, native
herd of cattle. The art of it
is where to put them. When
to move them on. The seasons

shift and alter at perception's
edge. All there is to do is
begin at the beginning,
to not be lulled and dumbfounded

by dogma or narrow, industrial
science, or be moved away
from how fields work with insects,
with flowers and rain, sun and beasts.

The Farm Faces Forward

The farm faces forward. Practicalities
are observed and acted upon.
If it's easier to sell butter by the kilo
than to push the same weight of meat,
then in comes the dairy herd and
things shift accordingly. The scales

balance.

Everything's an experiment in these
discordant, Brexit-weighted times.
The world seems stranger than it's ever been
on the surface. It moves so fast that soil
is an irrelevance, in certain circles.
Unworthy of complicated thought.

Balance

out of whack, shouted down on all sides
as fear sweeps through the halls where
power festers in unoxygenated compost.
Where the worms have turned on each other
and nothing breathes that does not breathe
fire or money. They will keep on doing so till

balance

returns to books and brains and hearts.
Until the quiet, relentless industry of soil
is recognised again for its ability to take
everything that seems separate and opposed
and unify it under the surface of the land
(this land, all land, any land). You cannot buy

balance.

It is only ever earned in the fertile scrum
of living together in each alchemical moment,
forging futures from the rot of shared history.
A farm faces forward. Spreads the muck
of living out in fertile handfuls. The pasture
is a place of beginnings as much as endings.

Balance

in the hay field. In high city towers.
Balance in fungal layers, in a cow's
digestive tract. Balance. The ladder
shifts as you climb it, with no wall
to rest against. Balance in the dairy.
In the bank. In crumbs of soil. In

the steady pulse of everything that lives.

Farm as Kaleidoscope

Imagine the farm as savannah
where plants grow as they will and fields
shift back in increments to the old

riotous states of abundance they knew
before small gods of money, order and obedience
ever yoked and furrowed thought.

Imagine the farm as kaleidoscope, where cattle
wander into view at unexpected angles past
free-ranging ponies, red deer, fallow deer, roe.

Somewhere in the pulse of woodland scrub,
quick-witted Tamworth pigs root up soil, sleep
or run from the farmer's exploratory rounds.

A militant flash of purple emperor, the alto purr
of turtle doves. All that is rare and extraordinary
in the chemical parklands of commercial farms

able to burrow under, nest in, glue eggs to the low
leafy scrub that whispers between light and shade.
Imagine the heavy clays of Sussex, inimical to crops,

verdant beyond measure, wildlife documenters
unable to keep up with each new eruption of life.
In the absence of large predators, imagine us

as curator, shepherd and, on occasion, wolf. Our hands
muddied with soil and caution. The frenetic music
of survival-at-all-costs slowed to an inclusive waltz.

The Soil Never Sleeps

The soil never sleeps.
In its voids, gas and waters gather,
waiting for thirsty roots to crawl
down motorway tunnels dug by worms.
For the spade. The plough.
The massage-press of hooves.
For the rain to run through its seams
and seeds to push up to the light.

The soil never sleeps.
It banks lives
in its soufflé stomach,
connects them to everything.
Even the dirt beneath fingernails,
the dirt caught in a mole's coat, sings
with a million microbes to the gram
of connections, growth.

The soil never sleeps.
Never slips into ideology or nostalgia.
It is place and purpose,
the perfection of decay.
A story that shifts
from mouth to mouth.
A crucible for rebirth.
A rooftop on another world.

Three Options for Farmers

Go up into the land beyond the plough
where a sheep's worst enemy
is other sheep, where the Beltie herd
roams as free as the jawbone walls
that map the centuries on Yorkshire's Dales
allow. Yes, here. Go here. The land
loses its man-made maps without animals,
without people huddling through a cold winter,
learning how to fail and fail better
together, dreaming of a landscape
       that lives in symbiosis
             with money and with love.

Or go down into the Southern valleys
to unblock drains that bleed brown
when the rains come heavy, to stop
the very best of the fields from running off
to make war with cars and roads.
Go out and sing with the corncrakes at dusk
in the spaces you have made for them,
       sacred in their stillness,
in the deceptive silence of abundant growth.

Or, perhaps, go into the towns and cities
laden with produce and stories,
your tongues ripe with carefully
disguised science, the bare
bone facts dressed in the muscle
of myth and memory.
Too much fact runs off busy people
like water from compacted soil.
Learn how to open them
to the seeds of ideas.
   Water them with stories.
    Watch them grow.

Reference

Acknowledgements

This book would not have been possible to write without the support of the Pasture-fed Livestock Association and the commission to be their poet in residence. I am equally grateful to the Sheepdrove Trust, whose support has helped me find the time to complete this book.

Enormous thanks and gratitude to the farmers who put me up on their farms: Neil Heseltine and Leigh Weston from Hill Top Farm in Malham, Yorkshire; Chris and Janet Jones from Woodland Valley Farm in Ladock, Cornwall; Fidelity and Martin Weston (and Matthew Lewis) from Romshed Farm in Underriver, Kent; Nick Miller and Sarah Dickins from Pen-y-Wyrlod Farm in Llanvetherine, Wales; Charles Burrell and Isabella Tree from Knepp Castle in Sussex.

Thanks also to:
Simon Cutter, who took me to the abattoir;
the Oxford Real Farming Conference, for whom I was poet in residence in January of 2017 (one of the poems written there gave this book its title);
Anne Garcin, Roger Garfitt, Jamila Gavin, and Karen Walker, for their invaluable advice and encouragement during the writing of the book;
Jo Sanders for her marvellous illustrations;
Philip Gross and David Constantine for reading the manuscript and sharing their thoughts on it.

Most of all, thanks are due to John Meadley, the chairman of the PfLA, who originally conceived the commission, and his wife Fiona, who have supported me throughout the whole process, even to the extent of letting me occupy the summer house at the end of their garden in temperate weather to wrestle notes and memories into poems.

The two lines that close the first section of The Abattoir on page 112 are quoted, with permission, from Wendell Berry's poem 'Rising'.

Glossary

Orf	A viral disease occurring primarily in sheep and goats
Smeuse	A hole in a hedge
Teg	A sheep in its second year
Woofer	A volunteer farm intern who works in a place for board and lodging

Adam Horovitz - Biography

Adam Horovitz was born in London and bred in the heart of *Cider with Rosie* country, where he still lives. His debut collection, *Turning*, was released by Headland in 2011. He was awarded a Hawthornden Fellowship in 2012, and was the poet in residence for Glastonbury Festival's official website in 2009. His memoir, *A Thousand Laurie Lees*, was published by the History Press in 2014. *Little Metropolis*, a CD of poetry and music, came out in 2015. In June 2017, Palewell Press published the anthology, *The Physic Garden*, edited by Adam and commissioned by Ledbury Poetry Festival. Adam is one of Ledbury Poetry Festival's Versopolis poets, was Herefordshire poet in residence for 2015/16 and is currently the poet in residence for the Pasture-fed Livestock Association.

Jo Sanders - Biography

Jo Sanders studied graphic design at GLOSCAT, then illustration at Stockport College. She has worked as an illustrator, artist, gardener and garden designer since. Her work has been exhibited at numerous Stroud Arts Festival exhibitions and at Stroud's Nasty Women charity auction. She illustrated *A Thousand Laurie Lees* (History Press, 2014).
https://www.facebook.com/JoSandersDesigns

Pasture-fed Livestock Association

The Pasture-fed Livestock Association (PfLA) encourages farmers to raise their ruminant animals wholly on grazed and conserved, bio-diverse pasture and forage, their natural diet - bringing benefits to the environment, to animal welfare and to human health.

The Association's Pasture for Life certification mark ensures that produce displaying it has been raised to the detailed standards that underwrite it.

Pasture for Life farmers can be found from Orkney to Cornwall and from Cumbria to Kent and they believe that, in the words of the American farmer-poet Wendell Berry, "Farming should be a conversation with nature."

Find out more at www.pastureforlife.org

The Sheepdrove Trust

The Sheepdrove Trust supports research and initiatives which increase sustainability, biodiversity and organic farming.

Palewell Press

Palewell Press is an independent publisher handling poetry, fiction and non-fiction with a focus on human rights, social history, and the environment. The Editor may be reached via enquiries@palewellpress.co.uk